PUSH
Through Your Pain

Your Pain Has Power

Natasha George-Bompart
Life Coach | Inspirational Motivator

Table of Contents

Acknowledgments

I would like to give special thanks to my dear Husband, Mark Bompart, for encouraging me to fulfil this milestone in my life. I want to also mention my dear mother, Olga George, my Sister Nisha George and Sis. Rosan Bompart for believing in my ability. They have borne witness to the supernatural breakthrough in my life and have experienced it in their lives as well. I want to pay special regards to Aunty Phyllis and Maria Thomas for their Spiritual and Career guidance they have accredited to me over the years of which, I am indeed grateful. To my Pastor, Dexter Daly, for his spiritual insight into my life as well; who had also prompted me to document the spiritual encounters and pen them in a book, namely (Push Through Your Pain - Your pain has power).

I say thank you to Rev. Ruth Lawrence, who encouraged me to go through with the publishing of this book, I would like to say thanks to my Brother-in-Law, Wendell Bompart for offering me guidance where it relates to setting up issues, since it is my First Book; this brings me to mention Adam, and the team at Dust Jacket, who helped ensure my project is up loaded within a timely manner, even under trying times as such as these, he is highly recommended by me.

At this juncture, I want to give special thanks to Ayana Chester Editing Services ACES TT acesediting.tt@gmail.com, for working tirelessly on my project to provide editing and graphic design services. I am very impressed with the level of professionalism and keen insight into bringing my dream to a reality; I must express my deepest appreciation.

Thank you all for helping me along the way, may God continue to richly bless you and your entire families, especially under our present circumstances. Thank you again.

Testimonial

I am living a grateful life, a life that has been infused with tragedy, pain, and victories. But through it all, I am convinced that the hand of God has been my rock and stay. Each day, I am reminded that I am living according to his time, and so I must testify openly about his hand of grace upon my life.

I am not using this as an opportunity to boast. On the contrary, I am simply taking the time to say thank you to my heavenly Father, his precious Son and the sweet Holy Spirit, who have been my strong defense even after the passing of my earthly father.

After his passing, I realized that my dependence on God has been magnified; this is why the godly encounters have increased as well. In fact, it doesn't matter what I face in life, for I must continue to be determined, steadfast and unmovable because I serve a great God. My God is quite aware of my humanity and that, as a result, at times I will be broken.

Therefore, the true purpose of this book is to acknowledge my real-life experiences, whether they were pleasant or not so pleasant. The short stories were intentionally included so that you could gain some spiritual insight into why our emotions play a pivotal role in touching the heart of God. I believe it is a hidden truth that most people are unwilling to explore or simply are unaware of and thus, only acquire head knowledge and never truly experience the supernatural hand of God in their lives.

John 14:21 – "He who loves me will be loved by my Father, and I too will love him and show myself to him." As I recap my life experiences, you will gain a better understanding of the importance of giving God our emotions. So enjoy and be blessed!

1

Spiritual Insight

Once you are a child of God, you will be subjected to some degree of pain. The degree of the struggle/ pain is for you to acknowledge that there is a problem that needs to be addressed. It is not a death sentence, though the process is unwelcome.

Tell me, who likes to suffer emotional pain? This includes shame, embarrassment, rejection, abuse, death of loved ones and the like. And yet, it is one of the sure ways through which God can ensure you attain your maximum potential and in doing so, he will achieve his goals. His ultimate plan is to prepare you to become a champion so that when you have arrived at your destination, you will be strong and not buckle under pressure.

This insight was confirmed by the Holy Spirit on 20th January 2019. Just before I opened my eyes early that Sunday morning, he impressed upon me floods of painful situations that I had to endure in the past as well as in the present. He deemed them all necessary, so that I could be brought to this pivotal moment in my life.

This is known as building momentum: when troubling, painful events help to fortify us into the next move of God, so that we can overcome/manoeuvre the enemies' tactics and schemes, in a more confident way.

So don't compare yourself with anyone, because not everyone is chosen to follow the same path as you. Let's put it this way: don't waste your energy or even be discouraged when your afflictions seem enormous in comparison to others, but rather celebrate that you are on your way to the top and the Father is doing his best to equip you in advance.

God uses this avenue to chart the course of our destiny because it is an important factor/ tool that plays a major role in our character development. Why, you may ask? Because it makes you into the choice vessel whom he can trust. He wants you to be able to weather the storms of life and when it comes, you will be qualified to handle life's difficult challenges.

To prove this, there is an account in Isaiah 54:16-17, where God confesses that he had created the blacksmith and the spoiler and that both can inflict pain. Yet he promised that no weapon that is formed against us will be able to prosper.

You see, God influences all his creation to respond to his will. Just a reminder: even your worst enemies are all subjected to the will of the Father and that's why the battle may seem unfair at times, but God's ultimate plan is to use them to make you into a vessel of steel; ready for battle when the need arises.

He wants us to be like soldiers, soldiers for Christ. And to also operate with Christ-like behaviour; not carnal behaviour, but from a spiritual standpoint. We must be mindful to be wise as a serpent and harmless as a dove. When he is finished with us, we will be able to stand at all times because we will become a weapon for his use.

Isaiah 54:16-17 New King James Version (NKJV)
16 "Behold, I have created the blacksmith
Who blows the coals in the fire,
Who brings forth an instrument for his work;
And I have created the spoiler to destroy.
17 No weapon formed against you shall prosper,
And every tongue which rises against you in judgment
You shall condemn.
This is the heritage of the servants of the Lord,
And their righteousness is from Me,"
Says the Lord.

That's why you won't be paralyzed into despair or buckle under pressure but rather, you will excel while others are caving in. So allow him to fashion you to become much more effective, fit for life and its challenges, by accepting his perfect will for your life.

2

Accept His Perfect Will

If you want to be effective, you must be broken effectively; that's how you will be able to gain strength, tenacity and agility. As a result, you will need no one but the sweet Holy Spirit because he will equip you with the necessary skills so that over time you could manoeuvre the enemy and his schemes. That's why God allows real-life situations to force you to activate your faith; in fact, this allows you to build momentum so that he in turn can demonstrate his glory.

"For the Lord disciplines the one He loves, and He chastises everyone He receives as a son." (Hebrews 12:6) So take your training, it is working out for your good, for he said. "For I know the plans I have for you, declares the LORD, plans to prosper you and not to harm you, to give you a future and a hope."(Jeremiah 29:11)

Therefore, if you feel discouraged at the moment, he is working it out for your good; there is a purpose for your pain. It hasn't been revealed to you at the moment but, in time, you will understand why it was necessary. "And we know that God works all things together for the good of those who love Him, who are called according to His purpose."
(Romans 8:28)

So rest assured that your Heavenly Father has your best interest at heart because he allows the pressure to intensify, to bring you closer to your destiny. Therefore, be encouraged that your victory is just a stone's throw away. Don't quit; you are a child of God and you were not fashioned to quit because you are a winner.

I know it will be hard to accept at this point but I must say it. You must give God thanks for your past, present, and current painful experiences because they can develop you into the chosen individual he wants to see in your future.

Before he blesses he must first break, so that when you have been tried and tested he could then trust you to positively deal with success. This is called character development. Your character is very important to him; he wants to ensure that he receives the full measure of his glory and that's why he spends a lot of time on character building. Don't be too anxious to attain but rather wait very patiently and work with him through the process. If he broke Joseph, he will certainly do the same to you and me.

3

Inspiration

While compiling the short stories for this book, I asked the Lord to pick a title and also to show me how to develop this book. He drew my attention to a single event that took place when I was about twelve years old. When I remembered the event, I laughed out so loudly, I nearly had an accident.

You see, back then my sister and I loved to play truth or dare. Unfortunately, she chose dare and came up with a plan. She planned to run across the road when a car was APPROACHING! Can you believe it? My sister explained to me very carefully, saying: "Just before the car approaches, time the car and then run across the road! YOU RUN FAST! Natasha, run fast, as fast as you can, before the car passes you".

As I watched her demonstrate, I looked on intently as she ran like a speeding bullet, safely away from the vehicle. I wanted to be successful too; I wanted to gain the approval of my sister, for I loved her so much. I wanted to do it better than she did; I was that determined.

I was scared beyond my wits, but I refused to let it show. My belief system was very strong that day. I honestly believed that God would protect me, so getting hurt wasn't an option. For as a child, I would often recite this scripture from Joshua 1:9, "do not be discouraged, for the Lord your God will be with you wherever you go". It seems that I didn't know about "Don't put your God to the Test". You see, I loved the Lord deeply and I believed he would protect me just like my Sunday school teacher had told me.

So I did it: I ran as fast as I could, escaping death in a heartbeat! Usain Bolt couldn't defeat me that day, for my small frame almost kissed the vehicle and I escaped, in a flash. My sister was so shocked that she willingly divulged the entire incident to our parents and I was reprimanded because I nearly scared my schoolmate's father (the driver of the vehicle I escaped from) to death.

The following day, the incident made headline news at my school as it had occurred the evening prior, when we had returned from church. I was so embarrassed because I had not behaved as I usually would; I thought to myself, who did this?

You see, my child-like faith/ belief system was being displayed at this moment and over the years I managed to use it on occasions that warranted the challenge. Mark 9:23 states, "If you can believe, all things are possible to him who believes."

It's simple, just take your belief in Christ with his word and give him your broken emotional state and you will then gain access to his supernatural power. I came to this realization one evening when I inquired of the Lord. I said "Lord what is wrong with me." He didn't hesitate to let me know, "check your belief system". ***This means I must believe in season and out of season.***

At this point I would like to draw your attention to an account in the Bible where the belief system is mentioned. Jesus wanted to know who the people said that he was, and he also wanted to know who they believed he was. It was Peter, in response to Jesus's question, who identified that Jesus is the Son of the Living God. Believe me, this information or knowledge is key and so crucial when faced with a dilemma.

We can know that we are never praying amiss but in fact, every time we fervently approach the King of Kings and Lord of Lords, we can rest assured that we will always prevail, simply BECAUSE he is in control.

Matthew 16:16-18 states: 'Simon Peter answered, "You are the Christ, the Son of the living God." Jesus replied, "Blessed are you, Simon son of Jonah! For this was not revealed to you by flesh and blood, but by My Father in heaven. And I tell you that you are Peter, and on this rock, I will build My church, and the gates of Hades will not prevail against it."'

That's why the impossible situation could be subjected to the will of God and become possible. This happens when you use your brokenness that is derived from your EMOTIONAL PAIN and let it be intermingled with your belief in God, of course! And then 'Boom': Power!! This is called the boomerang effect.

4

Push Through Your Pain

Matthew 27:46 reads: 'And about the ninth hour Jesus cried out with a loud voice, saying, "Eli Eli, lama sabachthani?" meaning "My God, My God, why have You forsaken Me?"'

Based on this scriptural excerpt, both the Father and Son were experiencing momentous pain. Matthew 27:45 draws a comparison to the Sun in the heavens to the Son of God. As the scene unfolds, it depicts the Son of God agonizing on the cross while the atmosphere mirrored his pain. God wanted to show the whole world that it was his Son who was taking the sin nature for all humanity and that's why the literal sun wasn't allowed to shine; it was darkened. This symbolism was essential because it showed the metamorphosis stage, which is from life to death.

All in all, it shows a pivotal moment in history which depicts the point of agony and suffering the Godhead had to endure. That's why the elements responded in such a manner because it signifies the day when the heart of God was broken. Both parties could have broken the agreement, even though the decision was carved in stone before the foundation of the world.

To win victory over death they had to push through their pain. The contract was set in motion when the first drop of Jesus's blood was shed; therefore, his death was a legal binding agreement.

It must be noted that Jesus didn't die from the effects of the cross but rather from a broken heart, because it would mean that for the very first time in his existence, he was separated from his Father - God.

Matthew 27: **51 states** "At that moment the curtain of the temple was torn in two from top to bottom, the earth shook, the rocks split." The separation proved enormously painful for God as well; this is depicted when God showed signs of displaced anger, by dramatically expressing his emotions to show how painful it was for him. You see, God could have easily killed everyone who had inflicted pain on his Son but he chose to display his displeasure openly by tearing the curtain in the temple, causing an earthquake and splitting a rock, raising the dead. The latter was a foretaste of what is to come when God will display his power to resurrect the saints and at the same time choose to handle emotional pain in a positive way.

Therefore, let us do likewise and positively push through our pain. We should take an example from the Godhead, for they chose to go through the process by acquainting themselves with humanity's grief/ sorrow/pain. Not only that, since the curtain or veil has been torn, we as God's children have the right to gain access to the throne of God at any time.

Now, we could gain access as a result of them pushing through their pain and thus now it is possible to know the Father through the Son. John 2:19, 'Jesus answered them, "Destroy this temple, and I will raise it again in three days."'

So, let us be encouraged, if he calls you to it, he will certainly help you through it. Just remember: never underestimate the power of the Blood and the Cross, because we are all bought with a price and the weight of it is voluminous. And for this reason, we must consider the power that is available and not lessen its use, rendering it ineffective because he died so long ago. In fact, the Blood and the sacrifice of Jesus are more relevant today than ever before.

Our Lord can handle it; the fact that he allowed it is all the more reason for you to give it back to him. This is the **boomerang effect**. We all experience pain. If you live long enough you will endure pain, be it mild, intense or severe. Our humanity is fragile, because if the right buttons are pushed, there is a possibility that the once majestic mountain could disintegrate into falling rocks, hurting anyone in its path. So, if you want to prevent this from occurring, it will be wise to channel your pain back to him. **This is the boomerang effect.**

For we know that we live in a fallen world that is filled with all manner of evil and if you are trying to live a righteous life for the King, rest assured you will be under severe attack from the evil one. So, therefore, you have to be prepared for war and not be ill-prepared in this battle called life.

In the same way, when you experience a toothache or even pregnancy, you will be told to push through your pain. When a child has a loose tooth, the parent would tell the child to take his/her tongue and push it out. Similarly, the nurse will tell new mothers to push with the pain.

So this means that your pain has a purpose. It has the power to move the heart and hands of God but we are taught to hide our emotions and to be strong and hold it together. Nonsense! Take it from someone who knows: there is a time and place for everything, including expression of emotions.

5

It's Okay to Express Yourself to the King of Kings

I have often heard: "God doesn't want to see your tears, he wants to see your faith." On the contrary, you can open up to God and express your fears and concerns to God in private. You can feel free to pour out your soul to him alone, when you seek him with all your heart. Jeremiah 29:13 states "you will seek me and find me when you seek me with all your heart." Frankly, this is an ideal environment for the breakthrough, just do it God's way!

It's okay to go ahead and cry but when you cry, don't cry for crying sake. Rather, give your broken state to the King of Kings and Lord of Lords. Just like Mary did with the alabaster jar: she mixed her tears with the perfume and wiped Jesus's feet with her hair.

Remember, these heartfelt emotions are experienced by all people but they can be turned into power. So go ahead and channel it by using it as a tool to ignite your faith in him. Simply doing this will enable you to experience supernatural intervention from God.

Why? Because God has a heart after you, he truly cares and loves you. His love is unconditional and he wants the best for you. That's why he will move heaven and earth - just for you! So go ahead and express yourself to him alone in private or public, whichever way suits you.

6

What is Pain?

It is a distressing feeling often caused by intense or damaging stimuli.

What is the Purpose of Pain?

Excerpt from:

https://www.beliefnet.com/faiths/christianity/galleries/6-ways-your-pain-has-a-purpose.aspx

Emotional pain has its rewards; the process is not welcoming but God uses it to help you identify that something is wrong that requires your attention. Trust me, the best person to address the situation head-on is God. He doesn't put you through trials/tests to spite you, but he wants the opportunity to help you because he wants you to discover and acknowledge your weaknesses so that you can depend on him for assistance.

Pain expands your endurance

The strength to endure testing and trials is the key to success and with this key, you will be able to build tenacity. If you want to see how much weight you could bench press at the gym, you have to gradually add more and more weight. In so doing you can discover your threshold, your limits. Therefore, it is necessary to go through emotional pain since it is all necessary to build endurance.

As an athlete, it is key to build your body for endurance and perseverance. You will have to run hundreds of yards so that you could build up physical stamina to run an actual marathon. You will not have the endurance to run the complete course the first

time you train. You may run one mile, then two, or three and then four and maybe five and so on.

You see, over time your body builds up resistance to pain and you can now run an entire marathon. In the same manner, your past experiences help you to weather the storms of life because they harness the propensity to enable you to push through your pain. Why is this so?

Your body has pain receptors and your brain registers it as sensory data all the time and it is stored for future use. That is why most people find it difficult to get over hurtful events because the painful memories keep reoccurring in their minds. So, it would be wise for us to acquire God's help so that we could push through existing painful experiences, by giving it back to him. So, don't let it handle you, you handle it with God.

Pain helps build maturity

It's never easy to go through the chastening of the Lord but if you allow the process, it will cause you to be more mature so that you can view the world

differently. If you would look back over the years, you would realize that you have matured and blossomed into a vessel of substance.

The same applies to driving a car. I want you to consider the very first time you drove a car and then compare it to your present state. If you are honest, you would acknowledge that although it's the same person, your driving skills have progressed over the years and now you are more confident behind the wheel than before. Likewise, he wants to do the same for you on this journey called life.

Pain Teaches You What Pleasure Never Could

WHICH DO YOU PREFER: TO HAVE AN EASY LIFE WHERE YOU HAVE NO TROUBLES, OR ONE FILLED WITH RESILIENCE BORN FROM ADVERSITY? THE LATTER PERSON WHO IS WELL ACQUAINTED WITH LIFE'S ILLS WILL BE MORE PREPARED FOR THE REAL WORLD THAN THE PERSON WHO ISN'T. BECAUSE PAIN TEACHES WHAT PLEASURE WILL NOT.

Pain makes you aware of how much you need the Lord, and that's why it is absolutely necessary to channel your focus towards him. In this way, your despair will turn into hope and hope into faith. Your continuous reliance on him would cause you to become much closer to him.

Don't strive to live this life without pain or try to avoid pain altogether because repelling the effects of pain will not help you in your future experiences that pain will bring. Therefore, if you want to be well equipped, don't feel sorry for yourself whenever you experience pain, because pain produces strength and foresight. By not appreciating its purpose, you will sabotage your purpose and be left with a void of not attaining your goal. In fact, it will hinder you from being a product of self-actualization.

Pain is the price for a greater reward.

Where there is much trouble and turmoil, we can rest assured that we will attain the blessings of the Lord if we continue to persevere. According to 2 Corinthians 4:16-17 (NIV): "For our light and momentary troubles are achieving for us an eternal glory that far outweighs them all."

Find the purpose behind your pain

"CONSIDER IT PURE JOY, MY BROTHERS AND SISTERS, WHENEVER YOU FACE TRIALS OF MANY KINDS BECAUSE YOU KNOW THAT THE TESTING OF YOUR FAITH PRODUCES PERSEVERANCE. LET PERSEVERANCE FINISH ITS WORK SO THAT YOU MAY BE MATURE AND COMPLETE, NOT LACKING ANYTHING" *(James 1:2-4, NIV)*.

Throughout history, many veterans of faith were redirected due to some sort of adversity. Even though they had to endure hardship, challenges, pain, lack and the like, they managed to embrace their faith and persevered. Can I say the same to you? Are you ready to find your true calling in life? Your current pain is a sure indicator that God's hand is redirecting your destiny.

7

What is an Intervention?

According to the Cambridge English Dictionary, an intervention is "an action taken to intentionally become involved in a difficult situation, to improve it or prevent it from getting worse."

So many times in our lives, we find ourselves faced with a dilemma, which would require the hand of God to deliver us. Sometimes we are cornered or even placed in a precarious position that would require an intervention from God. When it's all over we would exclaim, "If it wasn't for God, I don't know what I would have done". Let's be honest, we all need a little help from the Creator at some point in our lives, and this fact would lead me to say that we are all dependent upon his mercy.

To gain a miracle or an intervention from the Lord, we ought to see the need to feel free to wrap our faith with tears at some point in time. It shouldn't be done forcefully but rather in a natural way, as the emotions move you to tears. Some people are not comfortable with expressing themselves in this manner and so chose to hide their emotions and be strong.

But I beg to differ. If you want to build intimacy with your creator, this is key; so much so, the Lord hinted how we can achieve this. He said, "But when you pray, go into your inner room, shut your door, and pray to your unseen Father. And your Father, who sees what is done in secret, will reward you." (Matthew 6:6) Therefore let us grasp knowledge so that we can experience a supernatural breakthrough.

So what is the recipe for an intervention? Be yourself in his presence, don't fake or hide how you feel. Go to him just as you are but you have to believe in him and he will come to your assistance. But every tear you shed in faith — shattered but trusting, gutted but believing — has this banner hanging over it: "The Lord is near to the brokenhearted." (Psalm 34:18)

MY PERSONAL EXPERIENCE

8

Abused by Teachers

Growing up as a teenager wasn't easy for me. I had a lot of challenges and frankly, they are too numerous to mention. But I will tell you that my Science teacher, as well as my Accounting teacher, both had it out for me. On one occasion, my Science teacher was so displeased with me that she took my copybook and slapped me with it on my head in front of my classmates.

Then when I was much older, my Accounting teacher accused me of being too friendly with one of her students, so much so that she accused me of looking for 'man' in her lessons class. However, the person she accused me of pursuing was my dear cousin who was struggling in the class and was desperate for my assistance since the teacher was not considered to be an approachable person.

These two separate events shaped my future. It wasn't so much that I intended to prove them wrong, but I wanted to show them both what I could do with my life. So I worked harder and harder each day, for I was a determined child. My drive for success was so strong that every time someone dared to remind me about my limitations - though I knew that I had many - I refused to accept their opinions because I knew then God was with me and he is still with me today. This is the reason why I will always succeed once I follow his will.

During my secondary school years, I was privileged to hear first-hand from a past student who managed to defy odds and complete her education to attain her a Master's degree. I am pleased to say I have done likewise.

When I completed secondary school, I attained a grade one (highest grade) in my Accounting exam, which was a huge accomplishment at the time. I wanted to contact my Accounting teacher and give her my wonderful news but unfortunately she had left the country. Later on, I happened to cross paths with my Science teacher and of course, I shared with her the news of my success. She was shocked, but if she only knew how well I continued to do after that, she would have been even more amazed. We should never underestimate the power and grace of God in children, who give their lives to him.

"But Jesus said, suffer little children, and forbid them not, to come unto me: for of such is the kingdom of heaven." (**Matthew 19:14**) I am indeed grateful to my God who has continued to show himself strong in my life.

9

He is in Control

On 17th September 2018, I dreamed that I had stayed home that day. When I woke up, however, I refused to comply, so what could go wrong did go wrong that day. I had had a horrible weekend (to protect those around me, I cannot disclose the nature of the unnecessary hurt that had occurred; all I can say is that I was in pain like a wounded mother). When I arrived at work, I realized the right side window of my vehicle could not go up; all my efforts were in vain. To make matters worse, I had forgotten my wallet and driver's permit at home! When I came to this realization, I panicked; so I took the day off.

Rain was falling heavily and I had to fix the window on my way home, so I needed cash immediately. This would call for faith, so I drove in my car to the financial institution to make a withdrawal but unfortunately, I had no money in the account. My heart sank into despair. I questioned myself: "so what are you going to do now?" Tears automatically flowed like streams of bitter waters as I cried inwardly. I went back to my vehicle in a defeated state as my mind explored over and over how I was going to fix the window by the next day. I had no cash available at home and my husband was at work; this realization made me cry more and I unconsciously gave it to the Lord.

Just then, the security officer called me back since the cashier had made a mistake and I was able to receive the cash. The cashier apologized and I cried even more. Prior to this event, I had spoken to this cashier before, and I encouraged her that God would come to her assistance. Her countenance was uplifted and as a result she remembered my goodness towards her. She, in turn, made some calls to my organization so that I could receive positive feedback and that is why she called me in a flash to receive my funds. Thanks be to God.

Within an hour after I returned home, my son's school called and asked me to collect him at school because he had had an accident. He had fallen in a puddle of muddy water. So all the events had happened earlier because God knew my son would need my assistance as well. God had orchestrated this entire event so that his prophecy concerning my life would be fulfilled.

For he is God and he proved to me that day he is serious about protecting his word. It states *in* JEREMIAH 1:12 AMP, "THEN SAID THE LORD TO ME, YOU HAVE SEEN WELL, FOR I AM ALERT AND ACTIVE, WATCHING OVER MY WORD TO PERFORM IT." He knew that my emotional state wasn't right for work that day so to ensure his word didn't go back to him void, he orchestrated the events so that I would be forced to take the day off. For he is in total control of all life and he is fully engrossed with all situations; nothing catches him by surprise.

Throughout the bible you will find numerous persons who unknowingly used their emotional state to touch the heart of God; for example, Hannah, Hagar and many more. You have to remember our Father God will show compassion for his children, he will move heaven and earth to come to the aid of his hurting child. The only difference with our heavenly Father is that you have to come through his son, who is the Christ. So once we become his, we are engrafted in him and, for this reason, when we are faced with an emotional situation, we have to give it back to him because according to this verse, your pain has power BUT YOU NEED TO ACTIVATE IT.

"Now unto him, that can do exceeding abundantly above all that we ask or think, according to the power that worketh in us," (Ephesians 3:20 KJV). So, therefore, I will continue to take you on a journey through my life experiences, where I had supernatural encounters. In these distinct events, I needed God to intervene and have mercy on my family and me.

10

On the Breadline

I was around 18 years old and I had been finding it difficult to gain employment. It became very distressing; it was so stressful that my mother suggested I attend the deliverance service at church on a Wednesday night. Although I had all my qualifications, I still could not get a job. I was employed at my father's company for a short period, only to acquire working experience, but once again I was back at home doing nothing. As I recalled, I had my work clothes ready so that if by chance I got a call, I would be ready at short notice; I was trying to activate my faith, yet still no call.

So while walking towards the church that evening, I turned to Mummy and said in frustration: "Is God in that church?" Little did I know, he was already there waiting on me! The church service was a deliverance service and the visiting Pastor, Pastor Bain, had told me that I was being blocked in the spirit. When he prayed for me, I fell to the ground with the power of the Holy Ghost.

I eventually got a job through a close relative at church who told my mother about an opening at her job. This was the first supernatural encounter I had, where I felt electricity flow through my body and I knew beyond a shadow of a doubt, God had moved mightily in my life that evening.

But this job wasn't to last for too long. After a year of working at the establishment, I was informed through a fellow worker that the Manager said that I should look for another job. She didn't want to tell me so herself since she wanted the conversation to be confidential.

This was a big pill to swallow. I was just starting to get accustomed to the workers, traveling to and from work, and it was a comfortable working environment without much hostility. But hearing this came as a shock.

At the time I couldn't confide in my mother since she wasn't in the country at the time. I had to rely upon my father and my four siblings for comfort and reassurance that everything will be alright. For the most part, I didn't know what to do; I didn't want to rely upon my father to support me since he had four other children to assist at the time. So I stayed up late at night to inquire of the Lord, but I chose to worship and adore him with praises and thanksgiving. Then the unlikely happened: I heard the audible voice of God.

His voice was cool and calm. He had a strong masculine voice and he was very clear and precise, while he gave me a word of knowledge. When he was through, I immediately turned to my sister and said, "I heard the voice of the Lord". I told her what HE said, just in case I forgot or believed it was a dream. This occurred at approximately midnight. This scripture came to mind: "Call on me and I will answer you, and I will tell you great and mighty things, which you do not know." (Jeremiah 33: 3)

The following day, my earthly father called me frantically and said "Natasha you need to leave your current organization and take up the present job which I am holding on to today." Isn't that God? Let God be praised as once again my pain was used to activate the hand of God in my life. It wasn't my efforts or someone else's. It was simply my pain mixed with faith in the God I serve. The pain was used to activate my faith to make God move because I was desperate. I knew he alone could change my circumstances and he did. PRAISE be to God whom I serve.

11

Destiny PUSH

After being gainfully employed, I was placed in a department to work. Firstly, I must say that being sheltered while growing up wasn't to my advantage as I couldn't fit in at all. Since I was new, no one wanted to show me the work; I was devastated. I was young and impressionable yet I wanted to prove myself. However, every effort I made led me to nowhere. At the time I was temporarily employed and as a result, my zeal to become permanent drove me to report the employee who was giving me resistance at the time.

My supervisor made it worse for me and I got more resistance from the staff. So I was alienated and I cried bitterly. I decided to work harder by staying back after work. An employee who was versed in the overhead line aspect of my job showed me what to do while the other employees were not present. After gaining this knowledge I managed to study the files and work backward.

Now this was a daunting task, as I had to learn and analyse technical drawings so that I could estimate them and eventually give customers a price. I eventually won the respect of my Supervisor. I became better than the person who refused to show me the work in the first place, and I was eventually promoted to a higher position. God be praised. So, take your pressure; it is a breeding ground for promotion.

Now I will let you in on a secret: the last word in the word promotion is motion. Thus, the more pressure is applied, the more force/ motion you will attain to push yourself towards achieving your goals. So, therefore, pain/pressure means progress. Remember you can't feel pressure/ pain if you are dead so take it as a gift from God, because he allowed the circumstance to help you to be pushed into your prophetic destiny. So while you are pushing, love yourself, don't feel sorry for yourself, because your pain has a purpose.

"And we know **that all things work together for good** to **those who love** God, to **those** who are called according to His purpose." (Romans 8:28) Take for example, a rubber band. The more you put pressure or the more you prevent it from releasing, the further it goes when it is released; it will go the distance.

12

Pain is a Prerequisite to Access Power

[20] Now unto him, that can do exceeding abundantly above all that we ask or think, according to the power that worketh in us." (Ephesians 3:20 KJV)

This is a true account of the power that can be activated when you channel it to the King. On one occasion, my husband was in the hospital as he was very ill. I had to make a lot of trips to the hospital, while also keeping up with duties as a mother and at work, so my daily routine was daunting. I thank God for my loving mother who assisted me; thank you, Mummy. But what brought me to the brink of frustration was when members of my church visited my home and gave me a mental picture of the likelihood of my husband not making it, even though I repeatedly mentioned that God would take care of him.

When they left, I was so sad and concerned. I remembered I put the kids to bed and I went into one of our bedrooms and took it to the Lord in prayer. I was hurt, I cried BITTERLY! I wasn't prepared to be a widow. I was only in my thirties and the kids were too young to lose their father, so I cried even more. I prayed while the tears cascaded down my face and then the most wonderful experience became a reality for me: I spoke in tongues. I felt a well of living waters rumbled in my tummy, my tongue became light and I prayed in the spirit. While I did, I could understand every single word.

While under the power of the Holy Spirit, I was instructed to tell all ladies that he is able. THIS IS the power I referred to previously: we are all emotional beings who can travail very easily, so we can turn our emotional pain into power. "And from the days of John the Baptist until now the kingdom of heaven suffereth violence, and the violent take it by force." (**Matthew 11:12**)

In the end, things turned around. My husband said it was about midnight when a nurse came out of nowhere and checked up on him. She administered the blood transfusion properly because he had had difficulty receiving the blood before. I am pleased to report that my husband is no longer in the hospital, and he is doing quite well. Thanks be to God.

I recall an incident where late one night I felt a pain on my left side. I was scared; I didn't want to leave home at 11:00pm to go to the Health Centre. So, I prayed to the Lord and when I fell asleep, I saw in the spirit that the Lord came through my room, which is located on the second floor. This time I didn't see his face but I saw his back. He was wearing a white long linen attire with a gold sash. He was strong and had a sense of authority about him. He had long brown hair that extended to his shoulder. He seemed awesome, as a real mature man.

When I saw him, I immediately spoke in tongues and I remember never feeling the pain again. Thanks be to God. I wanted to know why he turned his back towards me but sometime after when having a discussion with someone, I realized he had to because by his stripes we are healed. "But He was pierced for our transgressions, He was crushed for our iniquities; the punishment that brought us peace was upon Him, and by His stripes, we are healed." (Isaiah 53:5)

13

Blocked a Prophet

This is another account that left me in amazement. Both my sister and I would normally tune in to 98.1FM to worship God while commuting to work on mornings. While listening one day, we heard that a Prophet was coming to Trinidad. We were excited, so we decided to attend. Little did we know that the God of Heaven was waiting for us to arrive.

I didn't tell my sister of my predicament but decided to keep it to myself. I wanted God's opinion and I didn't want it tainted with my sister's usual response. I wanted God to advise me and yet I didn't want my business to be on the streets. How was it possible to hear from him without being publicly embarrassed? Was it possible?

When it was my turn to receive prayer, my heart was at a standstill but I waiting for my word from the Lord. Before he came to me, the Prophet was flowing, giving out word after word, to person after person. Then when he came to me, he stopped and started to move uncomfortably. He became frustrated with himself and then he asked me what I wanted the Lord to do.

I then realized that he was blocked in the spirit. I openly confessed that I didn't want the Lord to expose my business and God, being a gentleman as he is, stopped the Prophet from flowing in the Spirit. I then said to him "I want the Lord to give me direction." Then the Prophet began to speak, saying this is LIVING proof of what he saw in the spirit: that I will be writing for the Lord. He told me that I have a lot of projects in my mind to do and I should do them and forget all my current challenges; focus and get the job done.

Whenever this situation crosses my mind, I am always amazed at how the Lord works, for he sees into the future and brings it in the present. He is so wonderful.

14

Give Until It Hurts

While commuting with my sister one morning, I wasn't aware that the Lord was about to test me. He used my sister to redirect my thinking that morning. The Lord had impressed upon her to tell me that he wants us to give until it hurts. I was in disbelief and I wanted so much to think otherwise but he knew I was struggling financially. God spoke to my spirit and in response, I decided that I would give my last few hundred dollars. When I did this, my tears flowed automatically, like a river down my face.

I was then told to ask my sister for a note pad because he will speak to me at work. Again the Lord is true to his word because he spoke to me and every word came to pass. He also gave me a promise. I thank you Lord for helping me with my tithes issue; this was a problematic area for me for many years. It's not easy but it is necessary.

"'BRING THE WHOLE TITHE INTO THE STOREHOUSE, THAT THERE MAY BE FOOD IN MY HOUSE. TEST ME IN THIS," SAYS THE LORD ALMIGHTY, "AND SEE IF I WILL NOT THROW OPEN THE FLOODGATES OF HEAVEN AND POUR OUT SO MUCH BLESSING THAT THERE WILL NOT BE ROOM ENOUGH TO STORE IT. I WILL PREVENT PESTS FROM DEVOURING YOUR CROPS, AND THE VINES IN YOUR FIELDS WILL NOT DROP THEIR FRUIT BEFORE IT IS RIPE," SAYS THE LORD ALMIGHTY. "THEN ALL THE NATIONS WILL CALL YOU BLESSED, FOR YOURS WILL BE A DELIGHTFUL LAND," SAYS THE LORD ALMIGHTY.' (MALACHI 3:10-12)

15

Identifying the Time and Seasons

In 2012, I was faced with a lot of challenges. To be honest I was not mature at the time to handle life and what it brought. I was bombarded on all fronts: at work, at home and at church; the battle was fierce. I decided to take a day off to take our kids to school so that I could spend the rest of the morning period with the Lord.

Little did I know that the God of heaven was waiting on me to come to him. I worshipped him, I sang love songs to him and I adored him. Then he spoke to me; I heard the audible voice of God. How do I know it was him? It was based upon the conversation. He said: "Natasha, I love you, you are mine and I am yours. I have orchestrated this time to be with you. My son is coming back soon. I will give you the microphone and I will use you in a mighty way."

Notice there are five I's in his statement. This shows that the hand of God had orchestrated the entire event, not I. For he always says I am, then I am. WHAT IS THE MEANING OF THE WORD ORCHESTRATE? ACCORDING TO THE OXFORD ENGLISH DICTIONARY IT MEANS "TO PLAN OR COORDINATE THE ELEMENTS OF A SITUATION TO PRODUCE THE DESIRED EFFECT ESPECIALLY SURREPTITIOUSLY."

For God to get my attention he granted the evil forces freedom to operate so that he could bring me to the point of surrender to seek his divine will for my life. God knows what he is doing and he is in control of every aspect of our lives. In August 2018 he confirmed his word in a dream, in which I took the same microphone and enclosed it in my work bag.

This spoke volumes to me! It showed the condition of my heart because I had desired secretly to keep the vision and dreams for myself since the issues in my life were a deterrent at the time.

God had other plans which I wanted to stop from becoming a reality. He wanted me to remain focused, so that I could share his message to all who are willing to hear. The Lord Jesus Christ is ever so near and God wants all to repent and to share in his Son's glory. That's why he allowed me to feel some measure of pain so that I could be informed about the times and seasons. He doesn't want me to be distracted with the issues of life and miss His Son altogether. It's not about us. It's about gaining and sharing Christ, the lover of our souls.

16

Instructions from the King

I got a dream on January 1st 2018. As I recalled, the dream began when I was motionless on the floor. I was emotionally overwhelmed, defeated and for the most part, I had no more zeal left in me to continue. As I lay there, in my spirit I noticed the sky was moving. It looked like stained coloured glass: very bright and vivid.

To my amazement, I saw two golden baskets coming out from heaven and then I felt in my spirit the Lord was being birthed by Mary and that he was coming. I was excited and longed for his return. Just then I saw a man leaning towards me. He took me by my hands and lifted me as though I was physically paralyzed but, in the dream, I was emotionally paralyzed.

Then he turned his back to me and said towards the atmosphere, "I love you April". This was intentional; he turned his back to me to signify that by his stripes we are healed. He foreknew that this month would have been very challenging for me.

That month meant intense preparation for the Secondary Entrance Assessment (S.E.A.) which my firstborn had to endure. Unfortunately, I was at my worst. Thanks be to God, that he foreknew my future and thought it best to speak to my mountain; thus I was able to live and not die. Each day, as a rule, I would do likewise and speak to my tomorrows, month by month and especially the months that would be more challenging for me. It is working.

In the next phase of the dream, my Lord carried me to my kitchen stove at home. He positioned me away from the stove so that I was unable to turn it off physically. The stove became engulfed with fire, each burner spat high flames, and they were out of control. I became very concerned;

the Lord was not alarmed nor dismayed, but I was. He just looked at me and I, in turn, looked at him and said nothing. I looked at him and I became courageous and spoke to the flames and said, "You need to listen to Jesus, stop. Stop, you need to listen to Jesus." All of a sudden, the fire stopped and there were no more flames.

He then switched locations and carried me to my living room. He was positioned at the head table and I was positioned at the side of the table, more or less at the second seat. I was thrilled to be in his presence and yet I knew he wanted to tell me something of great importance. While I waited on him to speak to me, I recalled how I stood in total reverence. I believed it was two-fold. He did that intentionally, so that I will realize the level of respect I must have for him and he showed me the power he has over me and the entire world; he is the head of my home, he is the real boss.

He then placed his hand at my family pictures moving from one picture to another. And as though to choose his words carefully, so that he wouldn't hurt me, he then asked me a personal question. I answered slowly and when I did, he disappeared. Jesus is all-knowing and he is a man of few words but when he speaks, he speaks volumes.

He assumed the role of the righteous judge and gave me an honest ruling that would clear up a personal issue in our home. He is really awesome, for I no longer struggle with minor issues and I became more knowledgeable. Now my husband and I are progressing in our relationship, as Christ showed me that he is the head and my husband is after him. I am after my husband and I must submit to him, as I submit to my Lord in reverence.

The commandment- love the Lord with all your heart and love your neighbour as you love yourself, speaks volumes to me. FURTHERING THIS UNDERSTANDING, EPHESIANS 5:21-24 SAYS, "SUBMIT TO ONE ANOTHER OUT OF REVERENCE FOR CHRIST. WIVES, SUBMIT TO YOUR HUSBANDS AS TO THE LORD. FOR THE HUSBAND IS THE HEAD OF THE WIFE AS CHRIST IS THE HEAD OF THE CHURCH, HIS BODY, OF WHICH HE IS THE SAVIOUR. NOW AS THE CHURCH SUBMITS

TO CHRIST, SO ALSO WIVES SHOULD SUBMIT TO THEIR HUSBANDS IN EVERYTHING." AGAIN, IN 1 CORINTHIANS 11:3, SCRIPTURE SAYS, "BUT I WANT YOU TO REALIZE THAT THE HEAD OF EVERY MAN IS CHRIST, AND THE HEAD OF THE WOMAN IS MAN, AND THE HEAD OF CHRIST IS GOD."

The Lord is God and he knows how to speak to his children and will choose how to speak to us, for his intention is to guide and love his children. His nature is kind, loving, meek and all-knowing. I was impressed and when he disappeared, I felt as though I had experienced a great loss. It makes no sense to live this life without him.

17

To Be More Christ-like

I remembered praying fervently before I slept so my Saviour thought it best to intervene. HE INTERVENED TO INTENTIONALLY GET INVOLVED IN A DIFFICULT SITUATION TO IMPROVE IT OR PREVENT IT FROM GETTING WORSE.

Before this event, I had an inner question about 'position', at church, at work, in society and matrimonial status and the like. I questioned how some may have had it easier and folks like me would get the raw deal. But all this was a non-issue as the Saviour cleared up everything for me with this heavenly encounter.

As I recalled, my sleep was prolonged for about another minute, because I could sense I was prevented from waking so that I could experience this supernatural encounter. All I know, I was beckoned to attend a meeting in the spirit realm; honestly, I was compelled to fly to a destination I did know. The location was an open pavilion. It was rectangular with gold and bronze interior. It looked heavenly and yet simple. When I arrived, I came to a halt when I flew through an open entrance directly towards my Saviour. This is mentioned in Psalm 27:5 – "For in the time of trouble he shall hide me in His pavilion; in the secret place of his tabernacle he shall hide me; He shall set me high upon a rock."

Before he addressed me, his face mirrored my emotions. I wanted to talk to him but I felt in my spirit that he already knew my deepest feeling. I thought that I had no reason to explain my reactions because he knew me entirely since he was experiencing the same feelings I did. So explaining my reactions then would have been futile.

Despite all my faults and misgivings, he is still in love with me because as I gazed upon him, I could sense he was and is very much interested in my well-being; so I surrendered to his will very easily. Right away, he then addressed me by my first name "Natasha" and said "have a seat". I followed suit because a chair was already positioned for me at his right, about an arm's length away. Notice he did not call me by my last name nor by my maiden name, but by my first name. This speaks volumes to me, because he meant to say he is my friend, he is fully acquainted with me.

Then, I was allowed to witness another person entering by flight and when he arrived, he also stood directly towards Jesus. For a second, I got confused. I thought that I was looking at Jesus but I was mistaken. It was John, his beloved disciple. From the moment he entered, I perceived humility, meekness and gentleness; so much so that it mirrored Jesus and that's why I thought I saw Jesus twice. But he had disciplined himself to become Christ-like.

I believe Jesus wanted me to witness the spirit of John and the love they both had for each other because when he approached Jesus, he was lowly in spirit, meek, full of divine love and devotion. Jesus welcomed John closer to him. At that angle, I observed that John's face was somewhat battered, as though he had gone through excruciating pain. According to theories concerning John's death, he was arrested in Ephesus and faced martyrdom when his enemies threw him in a huge basin of boiling oil. He was delivered from death but later was sentenced to slave labour in the mines of Patmos.

If you are not aware, it was on this island in the southern part of the Aegean Sea that John had a vision of Jesus Christ and wrote the prophetic book of Revelation. The apostle John was later freed, possibly due to old age, and he returned to what is now Turkey. He died as an old man sometime after AD 98, the only apostle to die peacefully.

So Jesus confirmed that John was indeed tortured in that manner but is with Jesus in heaven. Jesus also wanted me to witness first-hand how he loved John and wants me to demonstrate his love to others. So, it may seem to be a simple wish, but honestly, the next time I am in his presence, whether in a vision or a dream, I want to be embraced in the same manner as John was. I know Jesus loves me but he wanted me to witness how devoted he is towards his children and now because of this scene, I too want to be transformed and become Christ-like.

Some food for thought: if John and his brother James (who were nicknamed by Jesus, 'Sons of Thunder') can be transformed, so can we also be transformed to be Christ-like. The vision then ended and I awoke, and it was time to get ready for work; it was approximately 3 o'clock in the morning.

18

Near-Death Experience

I had two near-death experiences on November 7ᵗth 2017 and November 28th 2018. The first was in a vehicular accident and the other was as a witness to a vehicular accident. The latter was the scarier of the two incidents because it could have been me, on that unfortunate day. I was delayed by the Cashier at my financial institution so I immediately told myself not to bother because maybe the Lord was preventing me from something. So I went along and gave her no resistance in completing the transaction. When she was finished, I left the business place quite happily, and in a hurry, not knowing that danger was lurking ahead.

I saw an elderly woman get knocked down in broad daylight. All I know is that it could have been me. I made a promise to the Lord that I will try my utmost best to listen to him and I will obey his prompting, and that's why I am writing this book.

But for the life of me, I couldn't help but wonder why he would allow me to go through this experience. I was frustrated because the incident played over and over in my mind and I couldn't help but wonder why it wasn't me. But he answered me not too long after. While fulfilling my usual duties at work, a customer fell ill! This customer had three complications: high blood pressure, heart problems and seizures. I was informed about him and I willingly proceeded to assist him by giving him water, so that he could take his medication. Then the unlikely happened: he collapsed right there in the office.

If God hadn't prepared me before, I believe I would have been a nervous wreck and would have cowered from the situation because it would have been too traumatic for me to handle. The customer had three seizures. The entire office looked on panicking, thinking the worst would happen but it didn't because I called Jesus's name so many times and I whispered "the blood of Jesus" in his ear. Thanks be to God that I didn't forsake him among my peers, but I honoured his Son.

After some time, the gentleman returned to the office and gave us a thank you card and said thanks to everyone who assisted him, including me. He was so kind and grateful.

The other incident was amazing as well. While I was in the accident, I was instructed how to manoeuver my vehicle as the truck collided with it. If I wasn't given divine information in that moment, my car would have flipped so many times, I would have been dead for sure. That's why I was so calm while the accident was taking place, because I immediately knew what to do.

God allowed me to escape death in a heartbeat; it was a miracle. If I had panicked, I would have been dead but the Lord directed my steps. I came out without a scratch. Psalm 23: 4 says "Even though I walk through the darkest valley, I will fear no evil, for you are with me; Your rod and your staff, they comfort me."

This accident occurred just before my 41st birthday and it was intended to kill me but the Lord had other plans for my life because once again, I had promised to do his will.

Just to let you know how serious it was: the left-side back door had a huge hole/ dent in it. I was told by the Evaluator and by a stranger on different occasions that they have seen vehicles receive less impact, resulting in persons' deaths; therefore, the impact was indeed classified to have been fatal.

19

Covenant Relationship

Our God listens to us and hears our deepest cries. The Lord is ever close to you and he knows how to save his children. On September 6th, 2018, one of my relatives asked to speak with me. She wanted to know if I was happy with my husband. To make a long story short, she wanted me to leave my husband. I, in turn, told her that under no circumstance was I going to let that happen. Both of us willfully got married and as a result, the Lord was in charge of our relationship. She should also realize this in her relationship and give the Lord time to work it out.

Leaving her that night, my heart was heavy. At the point in time our marriage was at its worst, but I knew we were meant for each other. So I prayed that night and went to bed, not knowing that the Lord had a message for me.

What I am about to write is no lie. That night I dreamt that I was walking and met two persons who (in real life) were giving me a hard time at work. They alerted me to look at my pants; I was wearing a soldier's pants. They were amazed and said "Natasha your pants!" When I looked at it, it was full of blood and when I looked at my right heel, it was bruised. Then I noticed I went to sit down to wipe up the blood but it was just flowing and flowing; it was the Blood covenant. I had another dream, where I saw that my kids were very happy. They were playing and this was a confirmation to stay married for the kids' sake.

The following day, the Lord saw it fit to deal with the same individuals. Now I realize how serious the Lord is with blood covenant relationships, like marriage, and that it shouldn't be entered into, without first counting the cost.

Everyone who is married must realize that they have entered into a blood covenant relationship, of which Christ is the head and, therefore, couples should strive to walk following his will for their lives. Thank you LORD for making this ever so clear to me. I am grateful for your love to my family and to me.

No Token for YOU, You are Not a Potential Mother!

Mothers' Day and Fathers' Day are both significant and should be treated with due care and diligence. Even potential parents ought to be honoured as well. However, it happened that I was overlooked. My sister was given a token of appreciation for being a potential mother and I was TOTALLY left out.

I had good reasons to feel rejected because, you see, I was the one who was religiously involved in the lives of children at my church and not my sister. Whether it was in Sunday School or Vacation Bible

School, I was there, while my sister played effortlessly at the keyboard.

This came as a blow to me and I cried my eyes out when it happened. I didn't cry immediately because I couldn't believe it was happening to me and the enemy used my sister's blessing to hurt me in this manner. I immediately told my mother the entire story and that I believed the act was deliberate. She told me that I shouldn't take it so personally but I did, and I went to the Lord in private in the comfort of my home.

There I poured out my heart and soul to him. Back then I didn't know God listens ever so attentively to his children, but I told him how much I wanted to become a mother. Today I am and I love my children so much.

Thank you, Lord, for answering my prayer. I am grateful for the experience because I have two lovely children in the process.

21

You are Not a Biblical Mother

Before I was married, I told the Lord that I would give up the chase for a boyfriend to await the man of his choosing and that when I got married I would like my first child to be a baby girl. It did happen this way: my husband and I had a beautiful baby girl on the 12th of November 2006 and we were overjoyed.

I honestly thought everyone was happy for us. I was so naïve while expressing my joys as a new mother to someone close. But I was made aware that I was not a 'biblical mother'. I was told that because I didn't conceive a boy first, my womb was not blessed. She went on to call persons' names who had conceived a boy child first. I was in disbelief: did it matter if it was a girl or boy? My heart sank and I couldn't believe my ears. She also went on to state that my husband would not have a seed after his name. Frankly, I wasn't thinking about that. I was simply grateful to be alive having lost my father while I was eight months pregnant and also having survived childbirth. This was very hurtful since I was recently married so I cried for a while because I couldn't believe a woman could be so unkind.

I took this pain to the King of Kings and Lord of Lords and gave him the facts. I thanked him for the girl child he had given to me and also for the boy child that he would bestow unto us. I rested my case, and my son was born on the 28th of July 2010, for we didn't take a long time to conceive again. The Father saw my need and responded quickly because he knew the urgency.

I am not bitter but I am better. I am thankful for persons who took it upon themselves to point out the facts to me; it just so happened that I knew exactly what to do with facts that would cause immense hurt. I am happy for the hurt because God used it to propel me into my prophetic destiny. That's why I would always encourage people to use your pain effectively, do not waste it. God gives us emotions for a reason and these emotions are to be used wisely. I am not upset now over it; in fact, I am blessed because of the incident. If it hadn't occurred, I would have been content and lost my blessing. Now I have two lovely children. Thank you, Lord, for the hurt and the wisdom to know that I should give it back to you.

22

Hagar Experience: Hungry Baby

Having your first child can cause you to do some strange things. I was craving for curry and at the moment I had no money on me except my bank card. I did not want to wait for my (dearly departed) mother-in-law to prepare lunch for me, since I didn't want to trouble her with my needs. I prayed to the Father in the name of Jesus and I said: "Lord, you took my father and now I am feeling for curry. Would you provide some money for me, please?"

I told my mother-in-law that I was going to the shop and I left with my umbrella. As soon as I left her home, a taxi driver pointed out to me that I had dropped some money on the ground. Could you imagine me with my big belly bending down in the road in shock? I saw 20 and 10 dollar bills on the ground and no one in sight to own up to it. I thanked the Lord on my way back from the shop. Thank you, Lord.

During my first pregnancy I wasn't conscious about my weight, so I wanted to eat everything in sight. Yet with my second pregnancy, I promised myself to watch my weight as I was greedy the first time around. I remembered going to bed with only a glass of milk. While sleeping, I saw someone in a silhouette frame. He was dressed in white and had a blue aura; he was glowing. I asked him, "Lord is it you?" and he said "It is I". When he said this, I awoke to find myself very hungry so I got up and went to the kitchen to eat. I realized that this pattern of limited eating was not good so I decided to change my thinking. Ironically, now my son is older and has a large appetite although he is as slim as a pin.

23

Godly Instructions from the Lord

While pregnant with my son, I contracted the flu and virus from my husband. I was so worried that I went to him and we prayed together. I was concerned so I told my husband that I am not feeling well so I am going to pray. When I was praying, I heard a male voice who said that the child was his. At that time I didn't know that we were having a male child and so I continued to listen to him. He said that I must do what I have to do and he will do what he has to do. Almost immediately an evil presence came in the room to torment me. At first, I thought it was my husband resting on my chest, but then I realized it wasn't him, so I continued praying and rebuked the evil spirit.

I am thankful that the Lord saw it fit to speak to me. I am an ordinary person who loves the Lord dearly. Based on his conversation, he quieted my soul as all children are a gift from him and he wants me to continue to do my part. I thank you Lord for assisting me through the years and I will continue to love you despite my obstacles.

24

Heaven and Hell Experience

This event occurred at the most difficult time in my life. As I recounted, my father had died when I was eight months pregnant. I was having his first grandchild and I was expecting to present the child to him but it wasn't meant to be. The most hurtful part was when someone, on hearing the news, came to visit my family. She was so moved that she asked, in a caring manner, "If Jesus loved you, why would he do this to you?" I couldn't answer her but I sang "Jesus loves me this I know, for the bible tells me so". My heart was sad and my soul was in despair but I knew she had loved my father. So I dismissed the actual question and focused on the fact that Jesus does really love me.

Nevertheless, some years later, I became very bitter with life, knowing that I was fatherless. I will admit that I was, indeed, too much to handle at times. A particular night, I remember asking God to show me the supernatural and oh boy, He did! The pain of losing my father had pushed me into the spiritual realm and it opened my eyes to realize that it doesn't matter, we must all forgive others; whatever the offense, we must forgive everyone.

I remembered saying my prayers before bed and I said, "Lord forgive me for my sins." The next thing I knew, I saw a man who approached me and said it was time. I asked him if he loved Jesus, just to test the spirit, and he said yes. Then I saw many people walking and they all came to an entrance. Each had the blood of Jesus Christ stained on their shoulders, so I followed.

When I walked through the door my eyes were in amazement. The colours were different there; they were alive, they were dancing. God knew that I am an artist and I would appreciate the colours and it would give me great pleasure to behold and so the dream continued. I saw Heaven as clean as a whistle. I mean, there was no pebble or rock out of place, no cabbage or bins on the street and the mansions were huge. When I say huge, I mean huge! I saw one as tall as a mountain and the other was small in comparison, yet it was still huge also.

The roman pillars were as tall as the mansion and they were all embedded in the mountain. The architecture can only be done by the hands of God. It was so majestic, beautiful and full of light, and it was a glorious sight to see.

Everything looked so well-prepared and ordered. I saw a maze and a tree of life. At this point I was flying and I realized that I was in Heaven, then I was overjoyed. I knew my father had just died and my new-born daughter was on earth but just knowing that I was free and in heaven, I wanted to give thanks. I wanted to stay, I was that overjoyed.

I was carefree and I thought to myself: "I have no bills to pay!" I wanted to tell God, Jesus, thanks and frankly, I was so free and happy, overjoyed, emphatically excited. I didn't think, "Oh, I am dead". I didn't care. I said out loud, "Oh God ah reach, ah reach!" I recall that I celebrated with overwhelming exuberance; I was making circles, making cartwheels. I was in Heaven but, in the twinkle of an eye, I was transported to Hell. Hell is not a place where you would like your worst enemy to be. When I awoke, I was terrified! I was so terrified, I cried and ran to my husband. What I am about to tell you makes me cringe to this day.

Hell is a very dark and dense environment and yet God allowed me to see how traumatic and terrifying it is by showing me a torture chamber. I wasn't being tortured but I was an observer. God allowed me to see by providing his Goldeneye, YES God does have a huge Goldeneye that glows in the dark; remember he is the Father of lights. Psalm 139:8, "If I go up to the heavens, you are there; if **I make my bed in** the   depths, **you are there**." Yes, he is everywhere.

As I recall, I saw about six or seven persons glued to a wall, they had no physical features but the inner core of their bodies was yellow and the outer body parts were red. As the flames intensified, it caused the physical frames that were already glued to the wall to lift upwardly. While this is happening they would all scream in unison but as the flames diminished, their groans also subsided while their bodies collapsed downward on the wall. They must experience this over and over and right now they are being tortured in this fashion, at this very moment, now and forever.

The Lord permitted me to view this horrible scene over and over, and I was horrified. I wanted it to end. I felt sorry for them, my physical body couldn't bear it. I wanted to leave but couldn't. I admitted to myself at that very moment that, indeed, Hell is a horrible place to spend eternity. I desperately wanted to leave.

My body had experienced the best and worst in the same night. Let me tell you that Hell wasn't meant for humans. Our souls were not designed for that purpose; we were meant to be with the Lord, not in Hell. If you love yourself, I would advise that you must make it your duty to forgive everyone. It doesn't matter what they did to offend you; we must forgive because Jesus will not forgive you and me if we refuse to forgive others. Matthew 6:14 says "For if you forgive men their trespasses, your Heavenly Father will also forgive you."

25

Christmas Ticket

On the 21st of December 2018, I had made plans with my supervisor for time off as I wanted to conduct business so that I could fix my vehicle. So, with a mad rush, I left work hoping to reach back within a reasonable time frame. It so happens, I drove into a street marked 'No Entry'; it was impassable during the morning period only.

I did not know that there was a mean police officer waiting for me and six other unfortunate drivers that day. When I realized that I was among the group my heart quivered. My happy Christmas mood went into a panic because I knew I was guilty as charged. But what surprised me is how the police officer approached me. He was mean like a pitbull and not only that, but he was the only one that day stopping so many cars. I couldn't believe what I was seeing, knowing very well I had to reach back to work on time. All I was thinking was that I might have had to apply for a half-day off!

I became upset, and was very annoyed with him. I said to myself, "Just give me a ticket", when the officer wasn't around but as he approached me, I pleaded in a frustrated tone, "Have mercy, have mercy Nah!!" When he left, I joined in conversation with the other driver, noting that the officer was showing off because it would take him a long time to process all of us. When he came to my vehicle, he said in a serious tone, "Take out your driver's permit and license and come out the vehicle."

I complied and when I came out of the vehicle, he noticed that I was dressed to kill. I was wearing a red dress and I was smelling good too. But besides that, when I gave him my documents, I prayed a quick prayer and sent the anointing alone with the said documents. Just then his mood changed; he was afraid and was behaving strangely as if someone was tormenting him. Suddenly he changed his mind and said that we were all going to get a warning that day and that the next time he would not be so accommodating, because he was the only officer patrolling that day. By the way the ticket or fee was valued $3000.00 per person.

When we heard the fee, I said "I don't have that money." We all said the same thing in unison and we exclaimed that we had no idea of the rule. After the lecture, the officer handed us back our documents but left me for last. When he did so, I said jokingly, "You have saved the best for last!" Then one of the drivers told me that she was jealous and I responded that she should not be. I knew that I had a partner with God and that the ticket was not in his plans for me that day because I pay my tithes. I had three other encounters in which each individual had mercy on me. Two of them were very funny and I do not mind if you get a laugh at my expense.

26

Your Friends Will Carry You But Won't Bring You Back!

This next incident was a blast. I had travelled to my work without realising that my license plate fell out in the road. I was involved in a vehicular accident prior which resulted in a cracked plate that fell off while driving. As I recall, it was my aunt who alerted me to the incident, since it was parked close to where she lived. So, during the day, I made arrangements to have it replaced. But I must tell you, there is a saying, friends will carry you but they will not bring you back.

It so happened that my good friend said that he would carry me to get a number plate which he did, but to install the plate the car must be present. He said that he would drive in front of me and I would follow. I was in disbelief. "Are you sure, you are not supposed to drive without a license plate", I interjected. He said, "No I will be right in front of you." So, I followed him, and soon enough, we saw a police vehicle along the way and he bolted, gone! He left me to fend for myself but the police vehicle just drove off. Along the way another officer stopped me. He was so upset with me and he told me to pull over, with sirens and all.

It was the worst feeling ever, I wanted to die. I had had an accident a few days prior and now everything was going downhill. "Oh Lord, what next?" I was sick to my stomach. I said a quick prayer but I groaned with frustration and murmured to myself. How I am going to come out of this one?

The police officer was upset and told me that I shouldn't be driving without a license plate. I said I was trying to get it installed, and I showed him the receipt. His mood changed somewhat and he asked me, in a very annoyed tone, for a sheet of paper and a pen. When I opened the car he heard gospel music playing and then his mood changed again. When I returned with the pen he was in a better mood. I had no idea where the place was so I asked him if he could direct me to the place. He hesitated and said he was busy since he was in civilian wear and he was already late because of me. I insisted because I didn't want anyone else to stop me, so he gave me his number and also escorted me to the place where I could fix my license plate. Imagine that! I can call him anytime for assistance because I have his number.

To God be the glory, great things he has done. He performs marvellous deeds for man and he is indeed merciful and loving. When it was all over, I told the Lord, "You are my Father and you are taking care of me". I felt hurt that my friend had abandoned me but it lasted a few seconds. When I went over everything, I couldn't help myself from laughing uncontrollably. But when I was interrogated it wasn't a laughing matter; it was shamefully embarrassing and I do not wish this incident on anyone.

27

I Thought Only Cats Had Nine Lives!

Another incident like this took place recently. I was stopped by another police officer after work one day. It was after a long and difficult day at work and I had a headache so I wasn't thinking logically. I made a bad drive and that evening, it so happened that police officers were anxiously waiting for lawbreakers and I happened to be one of them again!

As I was approaching, a driver told me that I was going to get a ticket. I remembered thinking, "Oh no, not again!" and I said a quick prayer to the Lord. When the police officer saw me, I knew it: this time I was going to get the ticket. But when he told me to drive up and park further up the road, I told myself, "I am not going to get the ticket."

When he approached me, he told me to take out my driver's permit and insurance and I complied. He asked: "Do you know why you are getting a ticket?" I said yes but that my (blood) pressure was high because I had a hard day and I explained what had happened. He said "So if I give you this ticket, your pressure will get worse?" I said "Well yes!!" This was so funny, I couldn't believe it. I was spared again and I went away with just a warning. God be praised. I love you Lord for saving me.

28

A Christmas Miracle

What I am about to tell you is the truth, I am not making it up. To further cement this incident, I have my mother as a witness. On the 28th of December 2018, my Mom told me that she would accompany me to the car inspection site the following day, which was her birthday. The due date to have the inspection done was 1st January 2019, and if non-compliant by that date, motorists would have to pay $5000.00. I was grateful to her when she agreed to accompany me because I knew I would have been a nervous wreck if she wasn't there. My work and life schedule was so demanding, it didn't allow me the time to get a coolant cover replacement, because I had too much traveling to do. My life was too hectic.

I was overwhelmed with intense frustration because I knew I had a coolant without a cap. In fact, someone had placed a foil paper over it - yes, a foil paper! Imagine on the day of inspection, I had a foil cap on, with a broken coolant cover! All of a sudden, there was a commotion in the yard and I was drawn towards it. The inspector was giving out chits and he mentioned that it made no sense if anyone was there that day if they were not ready. I turned to Mom and said I should go but she refused and we waited anyway.

I told my Mom, "Mom I need a cap for the coolant!" So, I asked her to go to the nearest mini-mart so that she could buy a juice cover but when she came back it was too big. I showed her the size and she hurried along to the mini-mart, but when she came back, she looked dejected. Then she pulled the coolant cap out of her bag and I was dumbfounded.

I sat in my vehicle in shock for minutes and I praised God openly. The storekeeper told my mother that he had the same vehicle as I and that he kept an extra coolant cover when he had visited an inspection site years prior. When I eventually visited him to say thanks, I told him that he had kept it for me.

I thank the Lord because days after, I noticed that the broken cap was in my bag and a gorilla glue was there also; I was too distraught to realize it was there. So God had a ram in a thicket just for me. The car was inspected and I have my certificate, to God be the glory.

29

A Bird to the Rescue

Before I end this book I want to reiterate the importance of pushing through your pain. I remember this next event as though it was yesterday. You see I fell ill on the 13th and 14th of September 2019. On the 14th however, I was bedridden and my head was pounding as if someone was playing drums on my head.

I took medication and still got no relief. While lying down with nothing to do, my mind pondered on a thought: "It makes no sense, give up the ghost." I was feeling weak and I had no energy remaining to do my usual housework. So I closed my eyes and I wanted to float away. Just then, I felt a strong force. It grabbed my attention and even though my eyes were closed I could sense the energy of whatever was approaching as I lay in my two-storey home.

God sent a bird to pass very closely to my windowsill to grab my attention because it scared me so that I could fight for my survival. That was all it took for me to get my willpower back. This may sound simple to you but to me, I am happy God remembered me and sent a little angel in the form of a brown bird to help me.

Thank you little bird for obeying God. For in this life we will all struggle with issues and misgivings but we must always remember to strive by pushing through our pain. Quitting is not an option.

30

Conclusion

Using your emotions to touch the heart of God is no futile task because his will and intention are to be a father to all those who accept his one and only Son, who is Christ. He is the Son of the living God and he is only a prayer away! Thank you for allowing me into your hearts.

It has been my pleasure writing these true short stories. I have more but to be quite honest it takes a lot of time and energy to put pen to paper but it has been a blast. I am thankful that I was wise enough to document my experiences, visions, and dreams in my journal and I will continue to do so in the future because I am not sure what topic the Lord will allow me to explore next. I am excited because I've always wanted to compile my life experiences.

I have many more experiences and I believe the Lord will provide me with more insight into other books. But as for now the words and expressions in this book were given to me by him, through the Holy Spirit. I am a firm believer in the Trinity who allowed me to experience visions and dreams as evidence to bear witness that Christ's return is imminent and therefore he will indeed collect his Bride.

He wants you to use this book as a guide for your personal lives so that you can tap into his power so that you too can become an overcomer. He is powerful and with him, you can move mountains; just use your emotions and push.

Then you will see what your EMOTIONS can do: move the Hand of God. I hope this book has been a blessing to you.